101 PASSIVE INCOME IDEAS

A PRACTICAL GUIDE ON HOW TO TAKE BACK YOUR TIME AND ACHIEVE FINANCIAL FREEDOM

Tom Red

*This book is dedicated to all the dreamers
and risk takers out there.*

CONTENTS

INTRODUCTION

"If you don't find a way to make money while you sleep, you will work until you die"

- WARREN BUFFET

This quote always resonated with me. Imagine a world where you don't have to work. Don't have to spend your time creating someone else's dreams. Don't have to be told when you're allowed to go on vacation...

Instead, imagine living a comfortable life, in which you get to decide what to do with your own time. You get to take back control and have the freedom to do whatever you want. Doesn't this sound amazing?

This is the dream for many people, including myself. So I went about researching all the different methods that I believed could turn that dream into reality. I wanted to know the secret formula which would create that dream life for me.

After years of searching, a couple of terms continued to jump out. Those were "passive income" and "multiple income streams". But what exactly do they mean?

Passive income is income that you generate without having to be directly involved in the process. This means we can receive money at any time of day or night with no added work required.

This is the opposite of what the majority of us do. The majority of us work in 9-5 jobs. For us the only way to make more money is through working longer hours or via a raise.

This is why passive income is a truly amazing concept. It gives us the opportunity to take back control of our lives.

If we can create enough passive income to sustain our lifestyles. Then we don't have to grind at our 9-5 jobs in order to make ends meet. Instead, we've now created a life where we're in control of our time. Allowing us the freedom to do the things we've always wanted to do.

You'll be glad to learn that it has never been easier to create passive income too. Thanks to the internet opening up the world. Everybody now has the opportunity to create some form of passive income stream.

That's not to say creating a passive form of income is going to be easy or a get rich quick scheme. Many of the methods I'll discuss can take time and a lot of hard work to build. However once created, you can utilise these methods for forever more.

One method might make you a small bit of money each month. However, once you start stacking 2,3,4 or even 5 extra methods on top. Now all of a sudden, you may be generating enough passive income that could sustain your lifestyle even if you were to leave your job. This is why multiple income streams are also so important.

Multiple income streams are when you have multiple forms of revenue or income that you receive. The more streams of income you have, the better right? Wrong.

You don't want to have multiple forms of income that aren't passive. Here's why... the more time you spend working for money, the less time you have to do the things you love.

There are only so many hours in a day. When we spend them all working, trying to make extra money, unfortunately something has to give. Be that the precious time we spend with our families or friends, or missing out on important life events. This can cause massive strains on our relationships and will leave us feeling burnt out.

That's not to say working hard isn't a very important business trait. However, would you not rather work smart?

You can do this by working hard to create an asset that will generate an income. However this asset shouldn't require continuous time or effort to maintain. Therefore giving yourself the potential to make money 24 hours a day, with the added bonus of not having to work any extra hours in order to receive this money.

That's why it's important to not only create multiple forms of income. But to do so in a way that is passive. That way you don't just get reimbursed with money but also your time.

I've created this book to be a reference guide that you can keep coming back to for ideas. It is split up into four chapters.

These are:
- *Buy Cash Flowing Assets*
- *Build Cash Flowing Assets*
- *Share Assets*
- *Reverse Passive Income*

I'll explain more about each of these methods at the start of each chapter.

Lastly, before you begin, I want to wish you luck on your journey. I am on this journey too. I hope this book inspires you to take action, to achieve your financial goals and ultimately gives you your time back in order to live the life of your dreams.

If you want to follow my work, you can find my blog over at timeovermoney.co.uk.

CHAPTER 1

Buying cash flowing assets

"You must spend money to make money."

- PLAUTUS

The first method of making passive income is by buying cash flowing assets. Basically this utilises your own money to make more money. This method can be truly passive as you are leveraging money and not time to return more money in the future. This is great if you have a lot of money to invest with from the start.

(1)1. Dividend Stocks

Probably the number one passive income stream out there is investing into dividend stocks. With this method you invest your money into stocks that pay dividends.

These stocks can go up or down in price. Potentially making you more or less money via capital gains. However, every so often these stocks will pay you a share of their earnings as dividends for owning them. This means you can collect the equivalent of rent from your stock thus receiving a constant income from your holdings while maintaining a share of the overall capital. A nice totally passive form of income.

(2)2. High Interest Savings Accounts

High interest savings accounts are accounts where you lock in your money for a fixed amount of time. In turn, you receive a higher than market value interest on your savings.

The caveat is the longer you invest the higher the interest. However, this money is locked away and if you break your contract there are normally penalties to pay. So make sure whatever money you are putting into your high interest savings account you'll not need. That way you don't have to break your contract thus won't have to pay any penalty costs.

(3)3. Invest In Crowdfunded Real Estate

Don't have the money to invest in buying your own property? Don't worry, as a lot of sites now offer you the opportunity to crowdfund real estate. This allows you to own a portion of the real estate and therefore entitles you to a portion of the rent.

(4)4. Peer To Peer Lending

Peer to peer lending is a way for you to lend money to individuals and businesses. Just like a bank you receive interest on top of the loan repayments. Therefore over time you receive your initial capital back as well as well as making money on the interest you receive.

(5)5. Invest In Reit's

REIT's or real estate investment trusts are companies that own income producing real estate across a range of property sectors. This gives you a chance to own a share of valuable real estate without having to go out and buy, manage or finance the property yourself. These stocks need to pay out a minimum of 90% of it's taxable income as dividends. This means that owning REIT's stock normally generates a higher income yield on average than many other stocks in the market.

(6)6. Be An Angel Investor

If you have a lot of money available to invest, why not become an angel investor and buy equity in businesses. This means when your business that you've invested in starts making money, you receive your equity share of the profits. This can be a nice earner for relatively little time. However, there are risks involved. Business investment is highly volatile. Which means the business you invest in can also struggle and you aren't guaranteed to receive your initial investment back.

(7)7. Passively Invest In The Markets

Don't have time to pick what shares you want to invest in? Don't worry, there's a lot of sophisticated software to help you with this.

You can leave these tough decisions in the hands of algorithms and they'll pick the best stock to suit your profile. If you have confidence in the market to continue to return 10% on average each year and don't won't the hassle or time to pick your own shares. Then this could be a perfect solution for you to make money passively.

CHAPTER 2

Build Assets

"If you build it, they will come."

- FIELD OF DREAMS(1989)

This chapter explores how to make passive income by building assets. This normally means creating something of value which can take time or effort to set up. However, once the heavy lifting is done these assets can return steady streams of income with much less work involved.

(8)1. Affiliate Marketing

Affiliate marketing is perfect for bloggers or anybody with a following. When you are sharing content, you leave a link to the product or service which you mentioned in your content. If people click through this link and make a purchase, you then get a percentage of the sale. The best thing about this is that you don't have any work to do in creating the product or the service. This can be a nice little added income for those that are producing content anyway.

(9)2. Blogging

This requires time and energy to set up. This is why a lot of people outsource this part of their business to other people. However, once your blog starts getting an audience there are a whole range of ways that you can make passive income from the blog. The most common is through ad revenue. This is when people click on banner ads or other types of ads on your page. Ads alone will start to make you a nice little income on the back of your blog. Add in affiliate links, as well as paid posts. You could then have 3 to 4 different income streams just from creating your blog.

(10)3. E-Commerce Business

An ecommerce business is a semi passive way to make income. To get started it will require a lot of work and expertise to get off the ground. However, it has gotten easier to create a store and to market products than it previously has been. You can also hire a range of people to take care of your store set up, as well as marketing and the back end. A big aim is to try and have a product with recurring payments therefore you can start having a steady monthly income that you can depend upon.

(11)4. Dropshipping

Dropshipping is the process of being the middleman in an online transaction. Many people now create ecommerce stores and don't have a warehouse full of products. Instead they wait until they get a sale and then use that money to pay a 3rd party vendor to ship the product directly to the customer. You can hire a virtual assistant to process your orders and the best thing about this is that you don't have to rent or own a warehouse to store any of your products.

(12)5. Mobile App

A mobile app is a brilliant way to create a passive income stream. This can be through ads or through buying the app itself. There's a whole industry in it of itself of apps on the app store and the google play

store. If you're not technical you can hire someone
to create your app for you.

(13)6. Membership Site

If you have a following or are knowledgeable about
a certain subject then why not create a membership
site. This site allows people who've paid access to
view certain locked content. This creates a recurring
stream of income and you can hire a ghostwriter to
create your content to make it even more passive.

(14)7. Ebook Publishing

As you can see I'm utilising one of my own tips.
Have a book idea? Now you don't need approval from
a publicist to publish your book. You can publish it
yourself! This has opened up the market for everyday people to create their own books and provide
a lot of value for readers who previously wouldn't
have had the chance. It also is a great passive income
stream. As after you've written the book, if people
keep buying, it can make you a comfortable monthly
income.

(15)8. User Generated Content Website

Don't want to write the content yourself? Why not
create a user generated content site. This can have

any form of generated content you want such as opinions, reviews etc. This site you don't need to update as the users do that for you. You then reap the rewards from affiliate links or advertisements from hosting this content on your website.

(16)9. Contest Management Site

In a contest management site you hold competitions and draws for people who come onto your website to play. This generates traffic. Again from this traffic you can then create a passive income from either advertisements or display ads on your website.

(17)10. Subcontract Freelancing

Similar to dropshipping, you become the middleman in this transaction. People pay you for a service which you then pay someone at a lower price to do. You take the difference as profit. You could have your freelancers in place and can make this automated by spreading the work out between them.

(18)11. Network Marketing

This is a controversial entry as some see this as a pyramid scheme. As long as you're doing this ethically and not doing anything illegal then this can be a lucrative way to create passive income. Basically, it is a strategy in which you recruit new distributors and take a percentage of their sales. So for every sale they make because you recruited them you then get a percentage of it.

(19)12. Digital Course

This is one of the most popular forms of making money online at the minute. A lot of people are very knowledgeable on certain things. You can use this knowledge to create your very own online course. The best thing about it is after it is made, you can sell it anywhere. People will pay to gain knowledge on so many different topics and subjects so this market is still going to grow in the future. This is a nice passive income strategy as once the course is created it requires very little maintenance.

(20)13. Sell Digital Files On Etsy

Etsy is a very big marketplace for creators. Now you can sell digital files such as planners, calendars or trackers. People purchase your download and receive the download straight away. They can print it out or use the download anyway they please. Once you've created your product, you can then receive income from purchases with little upkeep or customer service required.

(21)14. Middleman In Retainers And Recurring Transactions

Do you have connections? Can you point people in

the right direction? Simply by solving a problem or showing a friend or customer a new product or service you could earn residual income from this.

An example would be a business in need of digital marketing. If you knew a person or business that could provide such a service, you could point this customer towards them. Because you referred them to a new customer, you can ask for a percentage of the profits the business receives from that new customer each month. You can think of this as being similar to in-person affiliate marketing.

(22)15. Lead Generation Website

This can take time to begin and set up. However, once you begin getting traffic to your website, you then can get them to sign up to your email list as leads. These leads can be sold to other businesses who would be interested in marketing to them.

You can hire an assistant to deal with the contract negotiations between you and the prospective businesses who are looking for these leads to make this more passive.

(23)16. Sell Photos Online

Do you take great photos? Or have you a photo that people love and adore? Well you can make money from this by selling your photos online. Content sites and businesses will pay for these rights in order to use them in articles, magazines or their own products.

(24)17. Be A House Sitter

People going on holidays or are out of town will pay you to look after their property. Basically, all you have to do is live out of different peoples houses, water plants and feed pets. This could be a handy form of passive income if you can work remotely.

(25)18. Buy An Established Blog

If you don't want to put in the grind of setting up your own blog with content, why not buy one instead? Many blogs will have an established audience which will make money each month from advertising without much added work. You could offer a lump sum to the owner and you then get the residual ad revenue from the site.

(26)19. Buy An Online Business

Again this step takes away a lot of the heavy lifting of creating your own online business. You have to do your due diligence to ask why this person is selling the website in the first place. However you can find some great businesses such as SaaS services where people pay monthly fees to gain access to different software and tools.

(27)20. Advertise On Your Car

Ok, this might not make you the coolest kid on the block but advertising on your car is a handy way of making passive income. Businesses pay you to have advertisements on your car as you drive around and gain them exposure. It doesn't require any extra work on your part but just being prepared to have your car's exterior changed.

(28)21. Sell Wordpress Theme

Millions of websites and blogs are hosted on wordpress. They use themes as a general layout for their site. If you know front end development or if you don't you can hire a designer to create a wordpress theme. Then sell this theme on the wordpress marketplace. You may need to hire someone for customer services or a FAQ's page to help non technical people deal with bugs and setting the theme up on their website.

(29)22. Sell Music

Why not create your own song? You could create the next big hit in the charts. Music and songs have now gone digital. You can create your song and distribute it online. The more plays, listens and sales the song gets the more money you make. If you create a popular Christmas song, then every year you can earn residual income.

(30)23. Advertise From Your Home

Is your house in a populated area? Why not allow part of your wall or create a billboard for businesses to rent and display ads to passers by. This way you may make additional revenue to pay off your mortgage or rent each month.

(31)24. Website Display Ads

By creating a website and getting a strong recurring audience to visit this site. You can utilise these visitors by making money from display ads. These are the picture boxes you see, that if you click on they'll redirect you to another website. These are good ways to create an additional revenue income however it can take a while for you to garner your audience first before you can utilise this method.

(32)25. Fulfillment By Amazon

Fulfillment by amazon isn't totally passive but it is as close to a passive form of income you can get. Basically, you create a product and ship it directly to Amazon for them to store and fulfil. When you make a sale of this product they'll take care of the shipping and fulfillment for you. All you have to do is keep an eye on inventory levels. You can hire an assistant to check stock levels and monitor sales to make this even more passive.

(33)26. Print On Demand

Similar to Amazon FBA this business model takes a lot of the heavy lifting away from you. You create a design and place it on products. Once you make a sale you then get a third party manufacturer to create and deliver your final product. This means you never have to touch or store the product yourself. Again I'd recommended hiring an assistant to check on sales and customer service to make this a truly passive income model.

(34)27. Sell Digital Art

Create a design or hire an artist to create digital art for you. You can then sell this online in marketplaces to people looking to buy digital art. Currently the popularity of NFT's are growing and collectors are looking to be among the first to acquire this new wave of digital art.

(35)28. Become A Business Partner

People have many strengths and weaknesses. Therefore it is sometimes better to partner up in business. You can lend your money to another partner who'll put the time in the business to manage it. Here you can get a share of the profits without having to put in the same amount of time and effort.

(36)29. Sell Graphics Bundles

Many businesses as well as people are constantly on the lookout for different graphics and designs to incorporate in their products. Here you can create your own bundle and sell it through a marketplace to constantly receive income, without having to physically send the product in the post.

(37)30. Audio Book Sales

Audiobooks and podcasts are major players on the scene. Many people now prefer to listen to books as they can perform other tasks while doing so. By creating an audio book, you only have to create the product once and you can make money from it for eternity.

(38)31. Self Published Physical Book

Again like audio books, amazon has made it really easy now for you to self publish your book. All you have to do is upload the digital files and if you make a sale they'll print it out and deliver it for you to your respected customer. Again this is a nice form of passive income as once you've created your product the delivery and fulfillment is taken care of.

(39)32. Sell A Font

Fonts can define a brand. Many films, music and businesses want their own or want to have their own unique features for their font. If you create your own font, you can sell this font on market-places or to big businesses for them to use through-out their corporation.

(40)33. Licensing Music

If you don't want to create your own song or music you can instead buy the license for a song. Here you can earn the residuals and money from the song without having to create the song yourself.

(41)34. Youtube Chanel

Creating a new youtube channel and trying to gain subscribers is relatively tough and can take time. However, once you've garnered an audience for yourself you can make a nice income from youtube alone. You receive ad revenue as well as being able to introduce ad placements into your videos as well. The great thing about youtube is that a video from 10 years ago can still get you views and bring you in money.

(42)35. Start A Forum

Create a forum of like minded people to discuss topics and share their opinions. Here you don't have to create the content yourself as your users will be creating the content for you. You can make passive income from ads on the site as well as creating paid memberships to access certain areas of the forum.

(43)36. Start An Exclusive Chat Room

People like being involved in exclusive groups. Chat rooms a bit like forums allow you to discuss ideas to people with a similar viewpoint. The great thing about making it paid is that you make it an exclusive membership therefore the information within these groups will be perceived as being more valuable. As you're not having to create content for these chat's they make a nice form of passive income for many people.

(44)37. 3D Printing

By buying yourself a 3D printer, you now can offer people the ability to create their own unique prod-ucts and services. By renting it out or by creating your own products you can receive another form of income for yourself.

(45)38. Virtual Tours

As the world becomes more and more digital. People now want to check out venues and places before actually getting there in person. To do this you can now buy equipment which allows you to take pictures that create a 3D image of the building or place you are in. Again you can hire out this service in order to create a nice little side income for yourself.

(46)39. Cv Templates

This may require a bit of design work at the start. However, once you've created your CV template, you can sell this digital file to people who want to create a strong CV. As this product is digital, it doesn't require any storage and the person receiving the item gets it straight away.

(47)40. Goal Setting Worksheets

Another digital product you can sell are goal setting worksheets. People like to stay organised and hit their targets. You can make it easier for them by creating a goal setting template to keep their lives in order.

(48)41. Excel Spreadsheets

The world is becoming more data driven. This

means more and more people and businesses are keeping track of more metrics. If you can create a spreadsheet template that a business or a person would find useful, they will happily invest in this to save time having to create one for themselves. Once you've created the template you can then sell this with very little maintenance costs.

(49)42. Software As A Service (Saas Website)

This may be for those of you who are technical or are prepared to hire someone who is technical. Basically, you create a tool or service which people pay to use. Each month you can make recurring revenue while the code you've created does the work in the background.

(50)43. Merch By Amazon

Amazon has created their own print on demand service called Merch by Amazon. Here you come up with a design and decide whether you want it on a t-shirt or hoodie etc. After this Amazon takes care of the sales and fulfillment. You can then sit back and wait to receive the profits you've made from the orders on your design.

(51)44. Royalty Exchange

Royalty exchange is an investing platform which

allows you to buy the royalty rights from music artists. Here, you can own the royalties to popular songs and albums. You pay the upfront price for the royalties and can live off the yearly residuals that song or music makes.

(52)45. Email Course

An email course is quite similar to a digital course only it is done via email. It entails emailing people daily or weekly with a new tutorial from your course. You can make this a paid course or free and make money from selling your leads to other businesses.

(53)46. Voice Over Royalties

Similar to royalty exchange but instead of music you can create your own voice over gigs. Once the gig is over you can still earn royalties for your voice overs and earn passive income from a one time job.

(54)47. Subcontract A Service Business

Are you tech savvy? You can become the middleman in a lot of these transactions. People are constantly looking for services such as cleaning, gardening or detailing to be done. You can offer these services on your website, take the order and then go out and hire someone to do the service at a cheaper price. You make profit on the price difference. This is the equivalent of dropshipping but only for services.

(55)48. License An Idea

Have a great idea? Instead of putting in the hard work of designing it, producing it and selling it. Why not instead license the idea out to another person. They can run with your idea and you can sit back and cash the cheques if they are successful with it.

(56)49. Price Comparison Website

You can create a price comparison site which shows how different products or services stack up within a certain industry. You can make passive income from this by either placing ads on the site or by allowing affiliate links to these companies.

People can then compare and decide which one is best for them. Then when they click your link to go to that product or service you get a percentage of the sale. Again you can do all this without having to create the product or service.

(57)50. Coupon Code Website

Similar to the comparison website, you'll garner an audience by providing people with discount codes and coupons. You earn your money from people using your codes which are affiliate links and you'll make a percentage of the sale without having to create the actual product.

(58)51. Review Website

Another idea which you can make money through affiliate links is via a review website. You buy and test the product or service and give your opinion. People then check out your review and decide if they want to purchase the product. If they do you'll get a percentage of the sale from your link, without having to be involved in the creation or delivery of the product.

(59)52. Selling Planners

People like being organised. A digital planner provides these people structure by giving them a plan on how they can achieve their goals. Like many of these products, it can take time setting up. However, once you've created the planner you can then sell this with very little upkeep required.

(60)53. Social Media Influencer

This can take time and hard work at the beginning to acquire your audience. However once you've gained a big enough audience on any platform, it opens up many opportunities to make a passive monthly income from ads or sponsorships.

(61)54. Give Opinions And Take Surveys

If you've free time while you are watching tv or just chilling out, you can make a side income by taking surveys or giving opinions. I only suggest this method if you have a lot of downtime and don't mind giving up 10 minutes during halftime in a match or during ad breaks. This means you can make money on your downtime for relatively little more effort.

(62)55. Play Video Games

Who doesn't like playing video games? Now you can get paid for doing so. New companies are happy to pay people to play their games in order to build an audience and gain traction for their game. You mightn't make your fortune doing this but it is a nice passive income if you're going to be playing video games anyway.

(63)56. Alexa Skill App

Alexa skills are addons which help the Alexa voice control experience. You can develop or hire someone to develop these skills and upload them to their store. Each month you can get paid recurring revenue when people download and pay for your skill.

(64)57. Shopify App Or Theme

Shopify is now the number one platform when it comes to e-commerce. Within shopify they have their own ecosystem of apps and themes which you can purchase. You can develop or hire someone to develop an app or theme to sell on their marketplace. With apps you can create recurring revenue when someone downloads your app onto their store.

(65)58. Install Monitoring Apps

If you don't mind sharing your privacy or your data, you can earn money by installing apps on your phone. These apps will monitor how you use your phone and what other apps you use. They make their money by selling your data to third parties. If you are happy with this you can make a side income by allowing these apps to run in the background.

(66)59. Patreon

Patreon is a subscription service for people to become patrons of content creators. This service provides an extra stream of revenue to people who create content. To make this passive your different tiers should provide options which don't require huge amounts of work. An example of this could be creating a tier which would grant access to a members forum or a chat room.

(67)60. Sponsored Instagram Posts

This takes a lot of time and effort to build up enough followers and engagement initially. However, if you are in the fortunate position of having an instagram following, you can utilise your audience by accepting advertising and sponsored posts. To make this passive you may need management to handle the different business offers, communication and the drawing up of contracts.

(68)61. Sell A Movie

Why not create a movie or documentary? This can require time to record and produce but doesn't necessarily have to be high budget. You can then sell your movie online for people to view. It may even get picked up by one of the major streaming platforms and you can earn residuals from it.

(69)62. Mine Cryptocurrencies

Cryptocurrencies have grown in popularity in recent times. This method isn't as profitable as it once was but there are still opportunities out there especially with the newer coins. You may have to invest in hardware however you can then leave your machine mining for coins while you have the free time to do what you want.

(70)63. Paid Newsletter

Why not create a digital newsletter in an area that you're interested in. You can set it up to go out weekly or monthly and charge people for the content. To make this passive you could hire a ghost-writer to create the content for you.

(71)64. Magazine Subscription

Similar to the previous example you can create a weekly or monthly subscription for your magazine. Your magazine can be digital or physical. You can spend your time creating content or you can hire people to write the content for you. Generating you a nice weekly or monthly income.

CHAPTER 3

Share or Sell Assets

"The more we share, the more we have."

- LEONARD NIMOY

This chapter looks at ideas for creating passive income via renting or sharing assets that you control. A lot of these methods are more physical in nature than that which we have covered so far. These methods can help utilise stuff you already own that may currently be collecting dust.

(72)1. Laundromat Business

This business requires an initial upfront investment to purchase your laundromats. You put them in an area where people can go to get their clothes washed. After you have your equipment you just need to hire someone to collect the money every month.

(73)2. Rent Real Estate

Again this requires a bit of investment for the initial deposit for the house. However, once you have bought your house or commercial property, you can then rent this out for a monthly income.

(74)3. Vending Machine Business

Like a lot of these forms of passive income this too requires an initial capital outlay. However, once you have bought yourself a few vending machines, you then need to find locations to place them. This can be hairdressers, hotels, manufacturing companies etc. Again you can hire someone to restock the machines and collect the money to make this totally passive.

(75)4. Rent Out Car

Have a car? Why not rent it out on days that you aren't using it. This way you can generate an income, even when the car isn't in use. This comes with risk as well as wear and tear so make sure you factor all this in when finalising your pricing.

(76)5. Rent Out Spare Room

Have a spare room that you don't use? Why not rent it out on Airbnb. This way you can make a side income by letting people stay in a room which would be going to waste anyway.

(77)6. Rent Out Parking Space

Live in a city or a town that has expensive parking? Why not undercut the daily rate of local car parks and rent out your space to commuters who would be more than happy to get a good space at a cheaper price.

(78)7. Rent Out Tools

If you own expensive tools or tools that are niche for a particular job. Why not rent them out? People would rather rent an expensive tool for a day or two rather than pay full price if they know they'll not use it more often.

(79)8. Rent Out Machinery

Buy a digger or other heavy machinery and rent it out to businesses and individuals who need it. You receive the rent income which can pay off the initial capital investment. Hire someone to lift or drop off the machinery to make it more passive.

(80)9. Rent Out Camera

Do you own a good camera? There are many people who are going on holidays or other events which will pay you to rent your camera for the day. This can make a handy side income for a gadget that you mightn't be using everyday.

(81)10. Bouncy Castle Business

You could invest in bouncy castles, then hire them out for children's birthday parties. Again this requires an initial investment to get started. Then you can pay someone to go, set up and collect your bouncy castles from the different homes.

(82)11. Car Park Business

Buy a car park in a place where a lot of people travel to work or to shop. This requires very little maintenance and makes you money on autopilot as people pay by the hour to park close to their shops or places of work.

(83)12. Self-Help Car Wash Business

This is another business which you can set up which

works on autopilot. By setting up self-help car washing bays, people will pay to get their car washed. While you can sit back and collect your money at the end of each month.

(84)13. Rent Out Garden

Do you own a garden? People are willing to rent space in other peoples gardens especially in built up neighbourhoods and cities. They can use this space to plant vegetables or do what they want with it. The best thing for you is that you can have a new stream of passive income for garden space which you mightn't have been utilising.

(85)14. Rent Out Belongings

People going on day trips to hike, ski, bike etc may need equipment for that day or two. They probably don't want to be forking out big money for an item they'll only use once. However, they can rent your items for the day and you can make passive income on items that are normally just collecting dust in the garage.

(86)15. Rent Out Caravan

This method isn't for everybody, as not everyone might own a caravan. However if you do, there's a good chance that during large parts of the year it is sitting idle. Why not in its downtime rent it out and make a nice bit of side income.

(87)16. Rent Out Bandwidth

You might be paying for a lot of internet bandwidth and not using it all. You can now rent out a portion of your bandwidth to others to make money back on your bill. This creates a nice little income for someone who doesn't utilise their full capacity.

(88)17. Storage Unit Business

In general we are all buying more and more products and items. A lot of the time people have no place to store these items. That's where a storage unit comes in. You create storage units for people to store their stuff. They pay you a monthly fee to hold it for them. This is a nice passive income business as it requires very little upkeep and can earn you a lot of revenue for just storing people's items.

(89)18. Rent Out Website

Do you have an old website that has a good google page ranking? You can now rent out your website to others who would love to use your website's domain or to those who don't want to pay all the costs involved in setting up their own website. Make a monthly fee for a website which requires little maintenance after setting up.

(90)19. Arcade Business

Similar to the vending machine business, an arcade business mostly runs on autopilot after the initial investment. This is a nice passive income business which doesn't require too much upkeep.

(91)20. Atm Business

An ATM business is another great way to make passive income. You find locations that people normally pay by cash such as barber shops, casinos etc and place your ATM in the store. Then you charge a percentage or a fixed fee for every transaction on the ATM. Every Time someone takes out cash from your machine you make money.

(92)21. Marquee Hire

Similar to the bouncy castle business, only instead you hire out your Marquee's. You'll probably want to pay a worker to go and collect the marquee from each appointment to make this method a more passive form of income. Marquees are normally in high demand for weddings, birthday parties and other social gatherings so you can make quite a nice return on your investment.

(93)22. Rent Web Hosting

Every website in the world requires hosting. These are special servers which store all the information of your website and provide it to visitors when they access your address. In order to rent web hosting you first need to acquire a server either by renting or buying your own. From this you can sublease hosting for websites from this server. You can make a nice income each month from web hosting which requires some technical knowledge to start but little to no work once it's set up.

(94)23. 24 Hour Gym

Another business idea which you can automate is a 24 hour gym. Purchase gym equipment and store them in a gym which gives each member their own access. People can come and go as they please while paying you a monthly subscription for this service.

(95)24. Renewable Energy

Create a wind or solar farm depending upon your location. These can generate a lot of energy which you can then feed back into the grid. Again this requires quite a bit of upfront costs, however check with your government to see if there are any subsidies or support for these purchases. Sit back and let nature take its course as you make money from the environment.

CHAPTER 4

Reverse Passive Income

"Do not save what is left after spending, but spend what is left after saving."

\- WARREN BUFFET

This method is about flipping passive income on its head. Instead of trying to create more and more passive income. We instead look at ways on how we can cut down our monthly expenditure.

In general I don't like lowering people's living standards. However, if there are ways that we can limit our monthly spending while still making the most of our lives then why not try it? Moreover, unlike the other methods in this book, we don't have to pay income taxes on these methods which makes them even more advantageous.

(96)1. Home Gym

Instead of paying for a monthly gym membership, why not create a home gym? This way it reduces your monthly expenditure as well as reducing commuting costs such as fuel or wear and tear on your car.

(97)2. Refinance Mortgage

By refinancing your mortgage, you may be able to find a better rate and again be fit to save on your monthly expenses.

(98)3. Cash Back Credit Card

When buying items, use your cash back credit card. You can use this when buying day to day items or essential goods. If you have a business, use your cash back credit card when paying for inventory or running costs. This way you can receive a small percentage of your money back for buying items that you'd have to pay for anyway.

(99)4. Cash Back Apps

Cashback websites and apps, give you cash back

when you shop on certain sites. So when paying for essential items such as groceries, pay for them via a cash back website and receive a small percentage of your money back for the next time you shop.

(100)5. Work From Home

With the way the world is, it seems like that more and more businesses are open to the idea of letting their employees work from home. If you currently don't have this benefit, why not ask your boss if this is possible? This helps reduce the daily travel costs, such as fuel or train tickets. It also takes away the wear and tear costs associated with your car.

(101)6. Pay Off/Reduce Debt

Do you have any debt outstanding? The quickest way to reduce your monthly expenditure is by wiping out this debt if possible. This cuts down the interest you are paying which will save you a nice bit of money each month.

(101+1)7. Reduce Entertainment

Thanks for making it until the end of the book. As a bonus I've included an extra method for you. This one is for people who have signed up for a lot of subscription services. Why not lose a couple and just focus on one each month? This not only reduces your expenditure each month but also gives you more free time to work on more passive income strategies. So it's a win-win!

CONCLUSION

Well done for making it to the end of the book. Think of this as a resource that you can keep dipping back into if you're ever in need of inspiration for passive income ideas. If you enjoyed this book and would like to find out more information, you can follow me over on my blog at timeovermoney.com. Thanks again for reading. I hope this book has inspired you to create your own passive income as this will allow you to have more time, to do the things you love with your life.

"All our dreams can come true. If we have the courage to pursue them."

-        WALT DISNEY